T0129524

Life
of
Leaves

A Book of
Poems
&
Short Stories

Emerson A. Murphy, Jr.

author HOUSE

AuthorHouse™
1663 Liberty Drive
Bloomington, IN 47403
www.authorhouse.com
Phone: 1 (800) 839-8640

Published by AuthorHouse 03/26/2020

ISBN: 978-1-7283-5773-7 (sc)
ISBN: 978-1-7283-5772-0 (e)

Library of Congress Control Number: 2020905782

Print information available on the last page.

To the Reader:

My hope is that this book illustrates the creative love of God. He has the power to lead us from the darkness of death, into greater light through Jesus Christ. Life of Leaves is an opportunity to witness the providence of God over your life. May the witness of the Holy Spirit give you peace and call you to your destiny in Jesus Christ.

Don't give up.
You are not alone.

May the Lord bless you today and forevermore.

~Emerson A. Murphy, Jr.

To My Wife:

I thank you for all the encouragement,
The grace and space you have granted me.
I love you as deep as the ocean,
And as wide as the universe.

Thank you for challenging me to reach higher,
And the depth of love you share towards me.
May God bless you deeply,
And His presence bring you peace always.

I love you.

CHAPTER I:

Fallen Leaves

Fortis

For the good of man weeps and tweaks
The old solitude of Rome.
Cunning with every attempt on his life,
Caladiums of joy prepares the way.
Will I never dream again?

Awaken the spring of twelve angels,
Sing the monastery oracle as high as the heavens.
Let this day be known as the moment of truth.
Pulsing minutes grave tension,
But the mule is an obsession.

Go therefore, to the earth's produce man of time,
Take what is weakened and make it strong.
Oast! Fly among the free-flowing winds of the clouds,
Jump to the fast lane.

With all moving towards east,
Will you turn west?

Stocky men of might drone past the mighty waters,
As if they were gliding across with such ease.
With many nights of reflection,
Great is the task before them.

Wilting minds of men divide the earth,
If he is willing, Death is a creepin'
Life is a callin', The choir is a singin',
Better gifts are given,
Brave men of heaven.

The March of Spring

Hope is what we live for.
What strife cannot break,
And water cannot purify,
We stand alone.

Hope is what guides us,
Through thought, word, and deed.
Creeds of doctrine,
Guns of night.
Whisper of smoke,
A silent slow breath of light.

As the soldier kneels before the alter,
Cries for mercy echo,
Among the hall walls of the sanctuary.
The choir sings with a melody of despair,
Time stood still.
A silent slow breath of light.
Whom shall I fear?

This is my destiny.
I shall let it come,
Let it be.

Redland Mystery

The journey of a million men has fallen to the will of one.
One who has begun a series of attractions and divisions.
A voice strong enough to beat the winds of thrust,
A vision so clear that all darkness and folly fades,
As if pixels of dust float in the air.
What confusion boils?

Shall life's torments of past failures ruin me,
Or make my current efforts stumble?
The journey of a million men has fallen to the will of one.

If I fly to the ends of the earth, will you guide my landing?

What desperate times have begotten us.
What can change the foreseen past,
Is the ever-present future.
Why trust me with this task of a million men?

An ear to listen to the heart with its many emotions,
A mouth full of wisdom to which men can learn.
A mind submissive to the will of the one,

Who Shepard's a million men.
Will you join me in this journey across
The Redland to middle earth?
Trust is essential in this walk,
And the pain goes away once we
Arrive at our destination.

The journey of a million men has fallen to the will of one.
One who has begun a series of attractions and divisions.
Will not she who slumbers in the dark come to light,
Or will the journey of a million men be proved waste?
The hour is upon us to make a choice in this march.
What will come of this?

Pride Street

When I was younger, all I ever wanted to do was be like my dad. Every day, I hoped to be with him. Help with whatever came his way. His faithfulness to provide for his family was always honorable. Time past, and I was old enough to travel with him.

In those days, I saw the work ethic of my father. Whenever we would drive together, he would play the songs of Marley. This was our bond, singing the melodies as we talked about the landscapes we observed. As quite as a mouse, my father explored the open road towards our destination and as I grew, I did too.

For most of his life, he worked the graveyard shift. I witnessed the strength of this man, imploring the winds of overwhelming labor on his shoulders. Though the labor was intense, he still pressed on. My father worked to make sure he provided what we needed and wanted, granting us time with him even when it was time to rest.

As the oldest of four, I had my ranks of responsibility. One of the major demands of being the older sibling was to take care of the younger ones. I took what I saw in my father and stood tall. Little did I know that power would consume me. I regulated, dictated, and managed. I wanted to show I had power and strength. This was the influence not of my father, but the people around me. See, for a teen, something about other teens makes them more trustworthy than parents. But it was the love of my father through discipline and guidance, that helped me see it different.

◆

Perfection was my poison. The illness can be learned and taught anywhere. Yet it seems that many take this road seriously. Nothing in this world will satisfy the burning pride of life.

For what does it profit a man if he gains the whole world and loses or forfeits himself?
-Luke 9:25, ESV

Fide

What is reality? What are dreams?
There are only broken ideas,
Leading to fragile pursuits.

A wondering soul,
Double tap, triple.

Peace calms us.
Heaven is near us with just a single prayer,
Weakness of heart shows humans are flawed.
Stubborn and persistent we drone forward,
Compassion does not drive our cars of dreams and hopes,
Nor does pride in our self-worth.

Our piece to this puzzle is but a simple one,
Yet we choose to play by an off-beat tempo.
In many ways, the drummer is our timekeeper.
CRASH!

Consider the song in measures,
Until faith heals our wound.

To Be or Not to Be

Selfless silver slides,
Without the maiden of barrows.
Surfing sights sighing,
Without the man of sorrows.
Do nothing,
Be everything.
Wanting more than what we are,
Parting waves of shifting fears.

Wisdom calls,
But we pant in wonder.
Joy brightens the sky,
Yet hearts are stone.
To be, to free,
Or shall we not be?
To be, is free,
So, let us be.

Life of Leaves

While sleeping in the cool of day,
A man was dreaming of a home.
Lights of night carried him,
Shadow of leaves gave him hope.

One day he wondered in the midst of the shadow,
Wilt was the might of his arms.
Trembling to embrace the fallen leaves,
His heart grew, but faintly pulsing.

Lights of night dimmed as the sky gloomed,
The man gathered the shadow of leaves towards him.
Though death approaches, he does not fear.
Yet, his eyes were full of tears.

Life as the man knew it was decaying,
He had little and gained nothing.

A voice cried,

"Man in the shadow of leaves, will you listen?
Come, listen to me and live."

Hearing the words of the Almighty,
He answered and now abides in the arms of his father.

The shadow of leaves is no more,
But the life of leaves carries on.

Lust Breathes

It was evening and the boy looked upward. The creaky floor echoed around him. His ears were lured to the front room. A sound of joyful screams appears. There was a woman's voice he could hear. She shouted, "More! More!"

Adventure was awaiting in the upper room. Interested in the sounds he heard, the boy walks forward. The woman's cry for more was sealed with her sighs of pleasure. The boy finally arrives at the door. Moving the knob to the unlock position, there was silence and fear. As the boy moves the door open, he walks through the door to find out what was this strange noise. Looking around, there was no woman to be found.

Confused with curiosity, the boy searched the room with great caution. As he enters in the last corner of the room, there the screams amplified. But all he saw was a TV. No one was around. So, the boy sat and watched for any signs of the strange noise. Right at that moment, a loud moan of sighs came again from a woman. He looks to the right, finds no one.

As he gazed upon the TV once more, the boy now sees a woman. She was naked and was with a naked man. Their bodies touched and motioned together. The boy was amazed at what he saw.

As the two continued, the boy's heart was racing. His body reacts to their motions. He feels anxious. His emotions express to him the breath of lust. Desire for the moans and touch awakened. The boy was no longer a boy anymore.

Footsteps at the front door peaked. The boy knew this was something he had never seen before. He concealed the actions of the day in his mind. The front door opens. He awkwardly runs from the upper room.

◆

Lives are ruined and families are destroyed because of lust. A boy only does what is set before him. So where are the fathers who will teach their sons? We need you. Our families need you. Your son, needs you...

> *But I say to you that everyone who looks*
> *at a woman with lustful intent has already*
> *committed adultery with her in his heart.*
> *-Matthew 5:28, ESV*

Wick Master

Flame doesn't wait for the spout,
Heat rises.
Timber lights flare besides the wick,
Masters of old cuddle the ends,
Sticks of skill.
Pressure admires secrets,
Dust blinds.

Bleak blades building families of wax,
While heat rises.

Reception of the Midnight Hour

A man was walking in the fields,
Smoke and dust covered the sky,
The world was gloomy and confused.
The man stopped as he gazed upward,
Noticing the darkness ahead he sought counsel with the light,
But the darkness had crippled him.

Among his peers, the darkness called his name,
Whispering great treasures and great pleasures.
He recounts his early days,
Searching desperately for a breaking point.

Where will he go to escape the chambers of the midnight hour?
The channel of dark calls to him were massive,
There is not a room of opportunity.

Wisdom was never there, but pleasure called.
Did he answer? Did he wait for the midnight hour of delight?

The darkness of night took hold of him,
Heart full of delusion,
He was a man that loves.

A King can grant the valley a century of peace,
But the heart of a man is the chamber of darkness.

Seek the King while the peace remains.

Wallow Calls of Nature

Today, I observed an oak tree.
See the root, see the leaves?
Base molded with silver dough,
Wool hung from the branches.

Withdrawn flakes of green pasture,
Surrounded by the sun.
The bark was heavy,
Dust covered the path.

Logs shifting patterns outward,
Lighter the oak, the darker the shadow.
Scattered bones cannot move as one,
But the wood of oaks bears much weight.

Cutting the tree, is life.
Lifting the branches, is purpose.
Planting the seed, is hope.

Flight Night

They stood tall without speaking any words,
Expression was movement,
Understanding was their language.
The two is greater than all,
Boarder barrier breakers.

Gestures similar in brokenness,
Yet the code of clay depicts their position.
A pail illustration of human rights,
Offering caves of darkness.

In blue daylight,
A man of gray particulars.
Without the mindless memories of the midnight hour,
The center of the crestline is here.

Gravity shifted when they kneeled,
Beyond self, they stood together.

Love moved,
Light was their language.
The two greater than all,
Brave believers of the sky.

Hands Built for Idols

The statement of highest regard among those whom I served is summed by their position of power. They carried doctoral degrees in various fields and much like them, I sought their approval. I too, wanted the position of wealth and the luxury of living like Mr. Jones. I enjoyed the presentation of greatness, a display of worldly influence. I desired to become like them.

Whatever whenever, was the motto of this company. People raved about the party, but rarely did I see anyone hurting because of the lost soul. As a young man, I had finally gained a position of wealth. Living like them, I became selfishly engaged. I trusted the lustful thoughts, gave into the desire of greed. What was supposed to be a one-time experience, became a war of the soul for several years. Doctors cannot save him. Neither his wealth. So, what of his soul? He is nothing to no one. He has everything, but not peace.

What is man to be without his fortunes? How can he survive? The war is heavy on the soul and damages the very life it claims to hold. Doctors are skilled but cannot cut the dry well of pain, nor the darkness of sorrow. So, what shall we make of tomorrow?

Put to death therefore what is earthly in you: sexual immorality, impurity, passion, evil desire, and covetousness, which is idolatry.
-Colossians 3:5, ESV

Skylight

Heights of the blissing day,
What like-minded people see in rain.
For reasonable thought,
But glory to gain.

Will the phantom of brightness blind the earth?
Forcing the father of night,
To plunge into girth?

Trickle tides tickle.
More than an old man's fiddle.
Twiddle-dee piddle,
Pumped with oil and griddle.

The skylight has spoken,
Human minds cannot understand.
Therefore, go and be well my friend,
For the day of sorrow has come to an end.

Flight of souls finally finds rest,
Flowing lights guide you home.

May the Lord find you well,
For the day of sorrow has finally come to an end.

Hummingbird of Veritas

Find the dream,
Fly through your imagination.
Thrusting and bolting through the air of illusions,
Find me.
Although time and space cannot be determined,
One thing is certain.
Death comes in all forms, shapes, and sizes,
Yet it does not speak about the nature of a man.
To live, yes, a man's life humbled by God's grace,
Truly this is the way destiny coexists with experience.

Intimate relations can cover two with one love,
But greed destroys their soul.
If the goal in life is to be humble and help others,
What is it that centers the mind of humans to sheer
self-pleasure?

If the heart of a mule is stubborn and does not change,
Why illustrate thy wisdom and kindness towards
ignorance?
If soon the world will end while our dreams become reality,

What is stopping the impulse that drives men into the hands of the Almighty?

I will find you and you will find me,
But only in time will dreams come into reality.

Hope and prayer are great friends of the believer,
Trust them and you will see the dreams come together,
Built and last forever.

Falcon and the Ghost

Floating in the air,
Circles of fire motion the sky.
The Falcon flies,
And the Ghost returns.

Traveling a distance to see green pastures,
He gained time.
Experts came to greet him,
The families of his home came before him,
He gained strength.

The Falcon was searching,
And the Ghost was struggling.
After three years of trial,
The tree of life gained new branches.

The Falcon called for his friend,
But the Ghost was gone.

He lives in eternity,
He leaves a legacy.

The Falcon flies,
And the Ghost returns home.

Daylight

Thank you for all the wisdom you have shared over the years. It may have taken me some time to understand, but I stand today because of you. I remember walking up and down 115th street to the local grocery store. I appreciated you prepping a meal for the family every day. The smell of bacon filled our nostrils. Saturday mornings became our time together. The family of one became a family of five. You were never a burden, but you were our greatest friend.

I remember your dedicated service in gathering the information needed for the Sunday bulletin. Fascinated by your strength, we watched with joy. Moved with direction, we were glad to help. I remember before breakfast, the call to have communion with God. My sister and I would have the David and Goliath series for devotion to read. We might not have shown our love for this moment, but we were deeply encouraged. The family of five, became a family of seven.

Morning after morning, you devoted your time before God. Praying, searching the scriptures, and even meditating on the goodness of God. We witnessed the faith of a great woman.

You carried us with love. Disciplined us with expected hands of service. We were deeply moved. We grew before your eyes. Your honor was our delight.

I remember the seasons of life and the leaves of wisdom you gave us. I didn't understand the roads before me. Inquiring to know, you pressed me to remember who's I am and who I am. Often you would say to me,

"If at first you don't succeed, try, try again!"

And just like Thomas, the engine of my heart was motivated to keep pressing forward.

To my shame, I challenged your leadership. Seeking to go my own way, I ignored the signs of wisdom you granted me. I became lustful, full of pride, and had idols all around me. I glorified evil, wanted to be like those who caused it. I was lost, confused, and distant. Yet you prayed for me.

I remember something you shared with me that I still read to this day:

> *Trust in the Lord with all your heart,*
> *and do not lean on your own understanding.*
> *In all your ways acknowledge him,*
> *and he will make straight your paths.*
> *Be not wise in your own eyes;*
> *fear the Lord, and turn away from evil.*
> *It will be healing to your flesh*
> *and refreshment to your bones.*
> *-Proverbs 3:5-8, ESV*

I admit that trust is a hard thing to do. Struggling to prove that I can do more than another, I failed to realize the call. My failure caused much pain, even to your eyes. Yet you prayed for me.

We were privileged to know you. In pain, you endured. Full of hope, you gave us a smile. Full of joy, you gave us your love. We watched with anxious eyes. You suffered and were granted freedom. Not once did you cry, even though we did. Not once did you give up on God, even though we questioned. Yet, you prayed for me.

Thank you for giving us a chance to say goodbye. I understand that it is time to decide. Therefore, I want you to know, that all your prayers were answered.

I believe God is real.

I believe God is one: Father, Son, and Holy Spirit.

I believe God the Father, created me for a purpose.

I believe God in Jesus, died and rose again for all my sins.

I believe God the Holy Spirit, is leading me into all truth.

Rest well Grandma, your crown is ready for you.

---

*I have been crucified with Christ. It is no longer
I who live, but Christ who lives in me. And the life
I now live in the flesh I live by faith in the Son of
God, who loved me and gave himself for me.*
-Galatians 2:20, ESV

CHAPTER II:

Branches of Hope

Letter to A Broken Soul: Day 1

The valley is often a place where pain resides. Destiny fails to carry our day. Hills of destruction distort our view. But the valley has a midpoint. It is where God wants to create something new. With the breath of life, these bones live. The Lord has a plan and purpose for you, beyond your pain.

The hand of the LORD was upon me, and he brought me out in the Spirit of the LORD and set me down in the middle of the valley; it was full of bones. And he led me around among them, and behold, there were very many on the surface of the valley, and behold, they were very dry. And he said to me, "Son of man, can these bones live?" And I answered, "O Lord GOD, you know." Then he said to me, "Prophesy over these bones, and say to them, O dry bones, hear the word of the LORD. Thus says the Lord GOD to these bones: Behold, I will cause breath to enter you, and you shall live. And I will lay sinews upon you, and will cause flesh to come upon you, and cover you with skin, and put breath in you, and you shall live, and you shall know that I am the LORD."

-Ezekiel 37:1-6, ESV

His word revives what is broken. The Lord wants to make His presence known in your life.

Today, allow the Spirit of God to lead you.

Letter to A Broken Soul: Day 2

Are you hurting? The Lord awaits your call. You may feel that you are so beyond repair, but the Lord is able. Will you come to Him?

And it shall be said, "Build up, build up, prepare the way, remove every obstruction from my people's way." For thus says the One who is high and lifted up, who inhabits eternity, whose name is Holy: "I dwell in the high and holy place, and also with him who is of a contrite and lowly spirit, to revive the spirit of the lowly, and to revive the heart of the contrite."

-Isaiah 57:14-15, ESV

Brokenness is necessary to make us whole. You are not a mistake, but you are His greatest masterpiece. The Lord desires to take what you see as broken and restore His purpose in you. He loves you.

Today, allow the Spirit of God to dine with you.

Letter to A Broken Soul: Day 3

Who am I? What is my purpose? What is my future? Often, many of us ask these questions of ourselves. Struggling to understand, some may have tried drugs, alcohol, sex, and even the job to bring relief. Yet the feeling of hopeless is there because none of these things bring peace to you. It is because of this very reason, Jesus wants to welcome you.

"Come to me, all who labor and are heavy laden, and I will give you rest. Take my yoke upon you, and learn from me, for I am gentle and lowly in heart, and you will find rest for your souls. For my yoke is easy, and my burden is light."

-Matthew 11:28-30, ESV

You have identity in Him. You have purpose in Him. You have a future in Him.

Today, invite the Spirit of God to teach you.

Letter to A Broken Soul: Day 4

Life is full of distractions and disappointments. Failure seems to cloud our minds. Fear drives us away from hope. The Lord is much stronger than your hurt. His love is much deeper than you can ever imagine. Will you trust Him?

"I am the true vine, and my Father is the vinedresser. Every branch in me that does not bear fruit he takes away, and every branch that does bear fruit he prunes, that it may bear more fruit. Already you are clean because of the word that I have spoken to you. Abide in me, and I in you. As the branch cannot bear fruit by itself, unless it abides in the vine, neither can you, unless you abide in me. I am the vine; you are the branches. Whoever abides in me and I in him, he it is that bears much fruit, for apart from me you can do nothing. If anyone does not abide in me he is thrown away like a branch and withers; and the branches are gathered, thrown into the fire, and burned. If you abide in me, and my words abide in you, ask whatever you wish, and it will be done for you.

By this my Father is glorified, that you bear much fruit and so prove to be my disciples. As the Father has loved me, so have I loved you. Abide in my love. If you keep my commandments, you will abide in my love, just as I have kept my Father's commandments and abide in his love. These things I have spoken to you, that my joy may be in you, and that your joy may be full."

-John 15:1-11, ESV

Today, allow the Spirit of God to speak to you.

Letter to A Broken Soul: Day 5

The world is filled with darkness, but the light is always shining on you. The words of death may attempt to hurt you, but they do not define who you are. Light is carried by the love of God and His word is true. When the world seeks to label, control, or destroy you, remember the words of Jesus:

And he opened his mouth and taught them, saying:
"Blessed are the poor in spirit, for theirs is the kingdom of heaven.
Blessed are those who mourn, for they shall be comforted.
Blessed are the meek, for they shall inherit the earth.
Blessed are those who hunger and thirst for righteousness, for they shall be satisfied.
Blessed are the merciful, for they shall receive mercy.
Blessed are the pure in heart, for they shall see God.
Blessed are the peacemakers, for they shall be called sons of God.
Blessed are those who are persecuted for righteousness' sake, for theirs is the kingdom of heaven.

Blessed are you when others revile you and persecute you and utter all kinds of evil against you falsely on my account. Rejoice and be glad, for your reward is great in heaven, for so they persecuted the prophets who were before you."

-Matthew 5:2-11, ESV

Jesus calls you blessed. He has heard your prayers and still awaits your call.

Today, let the Spirit of God comfort you.

Letter to A Broken Soul: Day 6

How long shall we suffer and endure pain? This is a question I've asked for a long time. But the truth of the matter is sometimes we have painful experiences in this world. Jesus guaranteed our freedom of death's hold and encourages us to endure. So, make your mark. Pursue the purpose God has designed specifically for you. All things you go through, good and bad, He will cause to work for your good. Satan will come to destroy, but Jesus has given you victory over Satan.

"Humble yourselves, therefore, under the mighty hand of God so that at the proper time he may exalt you, casting all your anxieties on him, because he cares for you. Be sober-minded; be watchful. Your adversary the devil prowls around like a roaring lion, seeking someone to devour. Resist him, firm in your faith, knowing that the same kinds of suffering are being experienced by your brotherhood throughout the world. And after you have suffered a little while, the God of all grace, who has called you to his eternal glory in Christ, will himself restore, confirm, strengthen,

and establish you. To him be the dominion forever and ever. Amen."

-1 Peter 5:6-10, ESV

Fight a little longer my friend. It's all worth it in the end. Today, let the Spirit of God establish you.

Letter to A Broken Soul: Day 7

Despite what your feelings may tell you, God wants you to overcome. He designed a plan that covers every step, breath, and choice you make. Broken souls are his to hold. You are not alone. Jesus was subjected to pain, shame, persecution, and ultimately, death. Yet He rose from death to life. The power of God is much stronger than your struggles and much deeper than your pain.

Everyone who believes that Jesus is the Christ has been born of God, and everyone who loves the Father loves whoever has been born of him. By this we know that we love the children of God, when we love God and obey his commandments. For this is the love of God, that we keep his commandments. And his commandments are not burdensome. For everyone who has been born of

God overcomes the world. And this is the victory that has overcome the world—our faith.

1 John 5: 1-4, ESV

Believe in Jesus, hang-out with Him by reading His word.

Today, allow the Spirit of God to grant you strength to overcome the world, just as Jesus did.

CHAPTER III:
The Garden of Peace

The Appeal

Man will die, but what remains is the truth.
Nothing is true.
Desires will fail, but what remains is the truth.
Truth is relative.
Heaven and earth will pass away, but
what remains is the truth.
My truth is all truth.
Pride will lead to death, but what remains is the truth.

What is the truth?
Jesus Christ.
Is it absolute?
Yes, from everlasting to everlasting.
For whom is this truth?
All of creation, throughout all time.

So, is it true that Jesus, died for sin?
Yes.
Why?

The Father of all creation saw the perfect opportunity to bring humanity closer to Him. He willingly gave his son, to cover all debt for all time. Jesus is the solution to sin, once and for all.

So, how does God's love exist if evil is present?

All evil is from the master of deception, satan. God's love is shown through the life of Jesus Christ. But man still has a choice. Sin is disobedience as well as the choice to reject the love of God through Jesus Christ.

So, what is the truth?

Jesus Christ.

Is it absolute?

Yes, beyond sequence and opportunity.

For all people?

Yes, beyond all land and sea.

Why?

All have sinned and fell short of the glory of God. But while we were in sin, God saw fit to bring us to Him.

How can this be true?

Faith in Jesus as Lord and savior is the seal of peace between man and his eternal destiny.

So, what is faith?

Confidently relying on the truth to set us free from sin, death, and eternal destruction.

What is the meaning of life?

Embracing the truth to live a life worthy of our calling.

How is this possible?

By following Jesus Christ. Submitting the day to God's way will allow the Spirit of God to bring victory over sin, now and for eternity.

What is the truth?

Jesus Christ.

Is it absolute?

Yes, today and forevermore.

But how can this be?

Satan came to destroy the image God created. The Lord, knowing the intentions of satan, granted time for grace to appeal towards His image bearers. The gift of God is the mercy found in Jesus Christ.

Why?

He loves you. Every person ever to walk the earth is made in His image. Corruption and sin carried us away from God. But He is calling us, even now. The greatest feast of all time is being prepared for the children of God.

So if you hear the voice of God, answer the call.
He is waiting.
The Lord wants to dine with you.
Will you listen?
Come to Jesus.

Will you accept Him?
Come to the arms of the Father.
Will you obey Him?
Come to Jesus and let the Spirit of God bring you from death to life.

Amen.

Printed in the United States
By Bookmasters